YOU SHOULD MEET

Jesse Owens

by Laurie Calkhoven

illustrated by Elizabet Vukovic

Ready-to-Read

Simon Spotlight

New York   London   Toronto   Sydney   New Delhi

SIMON SPOTLIGHT

An imprint of Simon & Schuster Children's Publishing Division

1230 Avenue of the Americas, New York, New York 10020

This Simon Spotlight edition January 2017

Text copyright © 2017 by Simon & Schuster, Inc.

Illustrations copyright © 2017 by Elizabet Vukovic

For information about special discounts for bulk purchases, please contact Simon & Schuster Special Sales at

1-866-506-1949 or business@simonanhdschuster.com.

Manufactured in the United States of America 1216 LAK

2 4 6 8 10 9 7 5 3 1

Library of Congress Cataloging-in-Publication Data

Names: Calkhoven, Laurie, author. | Vukovic, Elizabet, illustrator. Title: Jesse Owens / by Laurie Calkhoven ;
illustrated by Elizabet Vukovic. Description: Simon Spotlight /paperback edition.

New York : Simon Spotlight, [2017] | Series: You Should Meet | "Ready-to-Read." | Audience: Ages: 5-7.

Identifiers: LCCN 2016049021 (print) | LCCN 2016051498 (eBook) | ISBN 9781481480956 (pbk)

ISBN 9781481480963 (hc) | ISBN 9781481480970 (eBook) | ISBN 9781481480970 Subjects: LCSH: Owens,
Jesse, 1913-1980—Juvenile literature. | Track and field athletes—United States—Biography—Juvenile literature.
| African American track and field athletes—Biography—Juvenile literature.

Classification: LCC GV697.O9 C35 2017 (print) | LCC GV697.O9 (eBook) |

DDC 796.092 [B]—dc23 LC record available at https://lccn.loc.gov/2016049021

CONTENTS

Have you ever watched the Olympics and dreamed about winning a gold medal? Have you ever imagined running as fast as the wind or jumping so high that you touched the sky?

If so, you should meet Jesse Owens.

Jesse Owens had to help support his family when he was a child, so he worked in the cotton fields and shined shoes. But that didn't stop him from following his dream to become an Olympic track-and-field star.

Jesse went to the Olympics in Berlin, Germany, in 1936. The German government didn't believe that black people or Jewish people were as good as Germans. That didn't stop Jesse from proving them wrong and winning four gold medals.

If you like American heroes, then you should meet Jesse Owens!

Chapter 1
Alabama Cotton Fields

James Cleveland Owens was born on
September 12, 1913, in Oakville, Alabama.
He was the youngest of ten children. His
family had very little money. During the
winter, cold wind blew through the cracks
in the walls of their house. J.C., as his
family called him, was often sick.

J.C.'s grandparents had been slaves.
His own parents were *sharecroppers*. That
meant they lived on another farmer's land
and gave that farmer part of their crops as
payment. The whole family had to work.

When J.C. was seven years old, he was picking a hundred pounds of cotton a day. When he could, he walked the nine miles to and from the only school for black students. Black children and white children were not allowed to attend school together.

J.C.'s sister had moved to Cleveland, Ohio, and told the family that they could have a better life there. Soon the rest of J.C.'s family decided to move to Cleveland as well, where J.C.'s father got a job in a steel mill. Nine-year-old J.C. got on a train with his family and rode north.

Chapter 2
J.C. Becomes Jesse

In Cleveland, J.C. went to school every day for the first time. He was placed in a class with much younger students—first graders. When he was able to show the teacher that he could read and write, she moved him up to second grade.

That same teacher asked J.C. his name on the first day. He answered, "J.C." The teacher didn't understand his Southern accent and thought he said "Jesse." J.C. was shy and didn't correct her. From then on, most of the world called him "Jesse."

In junior high, Jesse worked in a shoe repair shop and delivered groceries after school to help his family. But at recess he **loved to run!**

The school's gym teacher and track coach, Charles Riley, noticed Jesse. The coach asked Jesse if he wanted to join the track team.

Jesse said yes.

Then Jesse remembered that the team practiced after school. The money Jesse earned was important to his family. He couldn't quit his jobs. So he went back to Mr. Riley and told him he couldn't join the team.

Mr. Riley agreed to come to school every morning to work with Jesse. He started getting up an hour early and running to school to practice with his coach. They became such good friends that Jesse started calling him "Pop."

Coach Riley taught Jesse to run like the track was on fire. That's how Jesse learned what became his famous high-stepping style of running. Coach Riley also brought Jesse to the horse races one day. The horses never looked over their shoulders

or from side to side. They ran straight for the finish line. That was how Pop wanted Jesse to run.

Pop also introduced Jesse to an Olympic hero, Charley Paddock, who had won three Olympic medals in track and field in 1920, and one in 1924. Jesse began to dream about going to the Olympics.

When it was time for Jesse to go to high school, some of Jesse's family wanted him to leave school and go to work. But his mother said that education was important, so he stayed in school. He continued to win races and set world records for his age group.

College scouts noticed the high school track star. Many of them wanted Jesse on their teams.

Jesse Owens, the grandson of slaves and the son of sharecroppers, became the first person in his family to go to college.

Jesse didn't get upset. He concentrated on being the best athlete he could be. With the help of his new coach, Larry Snyder, he got even better at running and jumping. Soon he was beating every other athlete on the track, and he became known at colleges all around the country. Jesse's nickname was the "Buckeye Bullet."

One Saturday afternoon, the whole country learned Jesse's name.

On May 25, 1935, Jesse took part in a championship meet in Ann Arbor, Michigan. In just forty-five minutes, he set three world records and tied a fourth. And he did it all with an injury!

Jesse had hurt his back. His back was so sore that he needed help getting dressed. Coach Snyder wanted Jesse to sit out the meet, but Jesse wanted to race.

Jesse took the field for the 100-yard

dash, and the pain disappeared. When the starting gun went off, so did Jesse. He crossed the finish line in 9.4 seconds, tying the world record.

Minutes later, Jesse tackled the long jump. He raced forward, stepped on the takeoff board, and jumped. When he came down at 26 feet 8 ¼ inches, he had broken the world record by more than half a foot. It would be twenty-five years before anyone broke this long-jump record.

Nine minutes after that, Jesse got into position for the 220-yard dash. He was so fast that he crossed the finish line almost 15 yards ahead of the second-place winner. His 20.3-second time broke another world record.

Jesse couldn't celebrate. Not yet. He still had to run the 220-yard low hurdles. When the starting gun went off, Jesse flew down the track and jumped over each hurdle ahead of the runners behind him. His time of

22.6 seconds set another world record.

Many people still consider this the single greatest day in sports history.

100 YD	9.4 SEC
LONG JUMP	26 FT 8¼ IN
220 YD DASH	20.3 SEC
220 YDS HURDLES	22.6 SEC

But Jesse had bigger dreams. He wanted to go to the Olympics. Everyone thought he was a sure thing to win every event he entered and come home with gold medals.

Then Jesse did something shocking: he started to lose races.

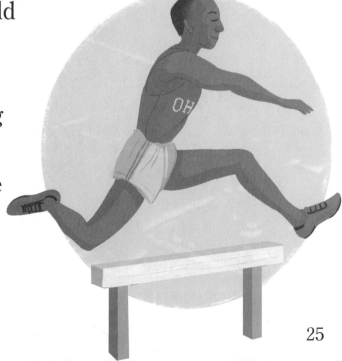

Chapter 4
Staying on Track

After he broke three world records, people from all over the country wanted to see the Buckeye Bullet race. Jesse went on to win the college national championships in California. But then things began to go wrong.

Jesse was racing too often and not thinking about what mattered most to him—his family. He didn't take good care of himself. He started to lose events.

Jesse realized what he had to do. He went home and asked Ruth to marry him. He also took a break from competing to work at a gas station to support his family.

By the time he started competing again the next spring, Jesse was rested and ready to race. In July, he went to the Olympic trials in New York City and easily won his three events. Jesse's dream of going to the Olympics was coming true.

The 1936 Olympic Games would take place in Berlin, Germany.

Some people believed that the United States should boycott the Olympics. Germany's leader, Adolf Hitler, and his Nazi Party thought many groups, including Jewish people and black people, were inferior. The German government had passed laws that forced Jewish people out of many jobs, and the laws made it difficult for Jewish children to go to school.

Jesse wondered if he should stay away from the Olympics. In the end he decided to race and show the Nazis what a black man could do. On July 15, 1936, he boarded the SS *Manhattan* in New York City to sail to Germany.

Hitler might not have liked black people, but the Germans couldn't wait to see Jesse Owens. More than 110,000

people watched from the stands as Jesse took the starting line for the 100-meter sprint. He crossed the finish line in 10.3 seconds. Jesse was the fastest man in the world!

Hitler was not happy to see a black American win the race. He never shook Jesse's hand or congratulated him, as was the custom for the leader of the country hosting the Olympic Games.

Jesse stayed calm. He had more races to run. The next day was the first round of the long-jump competition. Jesse did something very unusual—he fouled his first two jumps. His German competitor, Luz Long, showed Jesse where he should start his leap. His advice worked!

Jesse and Luz both moved on to the final round and the battle for the gold. Luz took the lead on his second jump, and then Jesse took it back. In the end, Jesse won the gold and set an Olympic record with 26 feet, 5 5/16 inches.

Luz was the first to congratulate his new friend.

By the time Jesse entered the stadium the day after the long jump to race in the 200 meters, the crowd was chanting his name in their German accents: *"Yess-say Oh-vens! Yess-say Oh-vens!"*

It was raining and the track was muddy, but Jesse did what he always did. He ran like the track was on fire and never took his eyes off the finish line. He won his third gold medal.

That was supposed to be the end of Jesse's Olympics. Then he found out that the US Olympic coaches wanted to add Jesse and his teammate, Ralph Metcalf, to the 4 x 100–meter relay race. Two other runners, Marty Glickman and Sam Stoller, were cut from the team.

Many people believed that the Germans had asked the Americans to cut the only Jewish athletes on the team. We'll never know for sure, but Jesse agreed to run the relay. He won his fourth gold medal, making him the first track-and-field star in United States history to win four gold medals at the Olympics.

He was an Olympic hero.

Chapter 5
An Olympic Hero Comes Home

Jesse came home an Olympic champion, but life for black people in the United States hadn't changed.

New York City gave Jesse a ticker-tape parade on Broadway. But when Jesse and Ruth went to a fancy dinner in his honor, they had to use the elevator that the waiters and maids used.

"When I came back to my native country, after all the stories about Hitler, I couldn't ride in the front of the bus," Jesse said. "I had to go to the back door. I couldn't live where I wanted. I wasn't invited to shake hands with Hitler, but I wasn't invited to the White House to shake hands with the president, either."

Jesse had received many job offers while he was in Germany, but most of those dried up when he got home. He struggled to make a living. He and Ruth eventually had two more daughters, and Jesse did what he could for them. At one point, he even raced against horses to earn money. People said it was beneath him, but Jesse pointed out that he had to eat.

Change came slowly. In a 1950 Associated Press poll, Jesse was named the greatest track-and-field athlete of the previous fifty years.

The state of Illinois asked him to help promote athletics. He tried to inspire young people the way his coach, Charles Riley, had inspired him. Then Jesse traveled around the world for the US government to promote sports and democracy.

In 1976, Jesse was finally invited to the White House. President Gerald R. Ford gave Jesse the Presidential Medal of Freedom, the highest honor a civilian can

achieve. Jesse went on to win many more awards and continued to promote sports and the Olympics, until he died in 1980.

Jesse never stopped fighting for what he believed in. He never gave up on his dreams, and his passion, determination, and hard work made him a hero.

Now that you've met him, don't you think you can do the same?

BUT WAIT . . .

THERE'S MORE!

Turn the page to learn a little bit about history, the Olympics, and some cool track-and-field facts.

Historical Hurdles

Jesse Owens rose to fame in the face of tragic events at home and abroad.

Jim Crow Laws

1877–1965

After the Civil War, the Southern United States created laws known as Jim Crow laws. These laws ensured that black people could not work, live, or learn in the same places as white people. The laws forced black people to use separate bathrooms, park benches, schools, hospitals, lunch counters, even water fountains. If black Americans broke these laws, they faced violence, fines, and imprisonment. The Jim Crow laws began long before Jesse was born and remained in effect until he was more than fifty years old. The civil rights movement finally caused Congress to strike down these laws in 1964 and 1965.

The Great Depression

1929–1939

When Jesse was sixteen years old, the Great
Depression began. This was a time of severe poverty
in North America and Europe. In the United States,
companies closed, jobs disappeared, banks failed,
and millions of families struggled to survive. At one
time there were fifteen million people who wanted
to work but could not find jobs. This time was
particularly hard on black Americans. Previously,
black people could find employment by taking
low-paying jobs that white people would not take.
Once the Depression began, white people would take
any job available. Even some soup kitchens (places
that serve free hot soup and other meals to people
who can't afford food) refused to serve black men,
women, and children. While the Great Depression
ended when the United States entered World War II,
the racism did not.

History of the Olympics

The Olympic Games started in ancient Greece in 776 BCE—that was more than two thousand years ago! Originally meant to celebrate the athletic abilities of young people, the Games also encouraged friendliness between the cities of Greece.

The ancient Olympic Games were held every four years while people were gathered for a religious festival. A group of all male athletes from around the country competed in different events—footraces, the long jump, the discus and javelin throws, wrestling, and chariot racing. The ancient Olympics continued for many centuries, until the Roman emperor Theodosius I banned them in the year 393 CE.

The Olympic Games began again more than fifteen hundred years later in 1896. After a visit to Greece, a French nobleman named Baron Pierre de Coubertin was  inspired to hold international Olympic Games. He hoped they would promote physical education around the world.

Women competed for the first time at the 1900 Games in Paris. Today, more than thirteen thousand athletes, male and female, from 204 different countries compete at the summer and winter Olympic Games. Athletes compete in fifty-six different sports and 406 events. The Games are held in a different city each time, in a special stadium built just for the Olympics.

After each event, the world watches as three medals are awarded. The athlete who finishes in third place receives the bronze medal. The athlete who finishes in second place receives the silver medal. Finally, the first-place winner receives the coveted Olympic gold medal. Out of thirteen thousand athletes, only a few get to "take home the gold."

• There are 8 running events in track: 100-meter sprint, 200-meter sprint, 400-meter sprint, 800-meter sprint, 1500-meter sprint, marathon, hurdles, and relays. (Women and men compete separately.)

• The shortest race is the 100-meter sprint. The longest is a 26.2-mile race called a *marathon*.

• It takes the average person about 4 ½ hours to run a marathon. The current world record for the fastest marathon is 2 hours, 2 minutes, and 57 seconds.

• A *triathlon* is a long race made up of 3 events: swimming, bicycling, and running.

• A *decathlon* is a contest made up of 10 events: 3 running races, hurdles, javelin and discus throws, shot put, pole vault, high jump, and long jump.

- The first recorded ancient Olympic event was a 600-foot-long footrace called the *stade*. It was the length of the stadium.

- A lap around today's modern outdoor track is a distance of 400 meters, or about 1,312 feet.

- Competitive sprinters train 20 hours a week.

- The average person can jump anywhere between 1 foot and 1 foot, 8 inches high. The highest high jump ever recorded was 8 feet, .45 inches.

- The length of an average person's jump is anywhere from 5 feet, 7 ½ inches to 7 feet, 6 ½ inches. The longest long jump ever recorded was 29 feet, 4.36 inches.

- In a 4 x 100 relay race, each team has 4 runners, and the teams compete against one another. Each runner runs a 100-meter sprint before passing the baton to the next teammate.

Now that you've met Jesse, what have you learned? Take this quiz and find out!

1. In which state was Jesse born?
a. Ohio   b. Alabama   c. Iowa

2. Coach Riley told Jesse to run like the track was on fire. What does that mean?
a. To plant his feet on the ground   b. To pick up his feet quickly
c. To stay low to the ground

3. Where did Jesse live when he earned the nickname the "Buckeye Bullet"?
a. Alabama   b. Olympia   c. Ohio

4. Jesse Owens tied a world record on May 25, 1935. He also beat how many world records that day?
a. three   b. four   c. five

5. Where were the 1936 Olympic Games held?
a. Greece   b. Russia   c. Germany

6. Which political party did Adolf Hitler lead?
a. Communist   b. Nazi   c. Unionist

7. What did Jesse struggle with after the Olympics?
a. employment   b. fame   c. loneliness

8. When was Jesse invited to the White House?
a. 1936   b. 1950   c. 1976

Answers: 1. b 2. b 3. c 4. a 5. c 6. b 7. a 8. c